HOUGHTON MIFFLIN LITERARY READERS

BOOK 1

HOUGHTON MIFFLIN COMPANY   BOSTON

Atlanta   Dallas   Geneva, Illinois   Palo Alto   Princeton   Toronto

Program Authors

William K. Durr, John J. Pikulski, Rita M. Bean, J. David Cooper, Nicholas A. Glaser, M. Jean Greenlaw, Hugh Schoephoerster, Mary Lou Alsin, Kathryn Au, Rosalinda B. Barrera, Joseph E. Brzeinski, Ruth P. Bunyan, Jacqueline C. Comas, Frank X. Estrada, Robert L. Hillerich, Timothy G. Johnson, Pamela A. Mason, Joseph S. Renzulli

Senior Consultants

Jacqueline L. Chaparro, Alan N. Crawford, Alfredo Schifini, Sheila Valencia

Program Reviewers

Donna Bessant, Mara Bommarito, Yetive Bradley, Patricia M. Callan, Marjorie Delbut, Mary Goosby, Clara J. Hanline, Gloria Hooks, Sannie Humphrey, Barbara H. Jeffus, Beverly Jimenez, Sue Cramton Johnson, Michael P. Klentschy, Petra Montante, Nancy Rhodes, Julie Ryan, Lily Sarmiento, Ellis Vance, Kathleen Ware, Sandy Watson, Judy Williams, Leslie M. Woldt, Janet Gong Yin

Acknowledgments

For each of the selections listed below, grateful acknowledgment is made for permission to adapt and/or reprint original or copyrighted material, as follows:

"Beatrice Doesn't Want To," by Laura Joffe Numeroff. Copyright © 1981. Adapted and reprinted by permission of the publisher, Franklin Watts.

"The Caterpillar and the Polliwog," entire text and some art from the book by Jack Kent. Copyright © 1982 by Jack Kent. Used by permission of Prentice-Hall, Inc., Englewood Cliffs, N.J.

"Caterpillars," from *Cricket in a Thicket*, by Aileen Fisher. Copyright © 1963 by Aileen Fisher. Reprinted by permission of the author.

"Clyde Monster," an adaption of the book by Robert L. Crowe. Text copyright © 1976 by Robert L. Crowe. Reprinted by permission of the publisher, E.P. Dutton, a division of NAL Penguin, Inc.

Continued on page 315.

Printed in the U.S.A.

ISBN: 0-395-47698-4

GHIJ-VH-96543210

Contents

3

Houghton Mifflin Literature
Millions of Cats

3.   Solving Problems

Houghton Mifflin Literature
Patrick's Dinosaurs

6.   Old Friends, New Friends

Helping Out

The Little Red Hen
A traditional tale
Illustrated by Jan Brett

Once upon a time there was
a little red hen who worked
very, very hard.

One day the little red hen
called to her friends.
"I have some wheat," she said,
"and I'm going to plant it."

"Who will help me plant the wheat?" asked the little red hen.

"Not I," said the duck.

"Not I," said the cat.

"Not I," said the pig.

"Then I'll do it myself," said the little red hen.

And so she did.

The wheat grew and grew.

Soon it was time to cut the wheat.

"Who will help me cut the wheat?" asked the little red hen.

"Not I," said the duck.

"Not I," said the cat.

"Not I," said the pig.

"Then I'll do it myself," said the little red hen.

And so she did.

Soon it was time to pound the wheat.

"Who will help me pound the wheat?" asked the little red hen.

"Not I," said the duck.

"Not I," said the cat.

"Not I," said the pig.

"Then I'll do it myself," said the little red hen.

And so she did.

Soon it was time to take the wheat
to the mill to make flour.

"Who will help me take the wheat
to the mill?" asked the little red hen.

"Not I," said the duck.

"Not I," said the cat.

"Not I," said the pig.

"Then I'll do it myself,"
said the little red hen.

And so she did.

Soon it was time to make bread
with the flour.

"Who will help me make bread?"
asked the little red hen.

"Not I," said the duck.

"Not I," said the cat.

"Not I," said the pig.

"Then I'll do it myself," said the little
red hen.

And so she did.

Soon it was time to eat the bread.

"Who will help me eat the bread?" asked the little red hen.

"I will!" said the duck.

"I will!" said the cat.

"I will!" said the pig.

"Oh, no," said the little red hen.
"You didn't help me plant the wheat.
You didn't help me cut the wheat.
You didn't help me pound the wheat.
You didn't help me take the wheat
to the mill.
You didn't help me make the bread,
so you won't help me eat the bread.
I will do it myself."
And so she did!

Spring Planting
by Marchette Chute

My garden seeds are coming up
   In the most surprising squiggles.
I planted them extremely straight,
   And then they got the wiggles.

One More Thing, Dad

From the book by Susan L. Thompson
Illustrated by Dora Leder

"I'm going out, Dad," Caleb said.

"Oh?" said his father. He was
making bread.

"Yes," Caleb said. "Can I take
an orange with me?"

His father gave him the biggest one.
"There you are, Caleb."

Caleb looked at the orange in his
hands.

"That's ONE," he counted.

"Yes, Caleb? Something else?"
said his dad.

24

"Maybe I should take a
peanut butter sandwich, too."

"Fine," said Dad. "You know how
to make that, Caleb."

Caleb made a big sandwich.

"That's TWO," he said.

"Hmmm. Some milk
would be nice with this
peanut butter."
"Help yourself," said Dad.
Caleb got the purple
thermos. He filled it with milk.

26

"That's THREE," he said.
"Maybe I should take
a celery stick, too, just
in case."
　　His father nodded. "Just in case."
　　He gave Caleb a green celery stick.

"FOUR," said Caleb.

Caleb put his things into a
big, brown bag. He looked into the
bag and counted everything.

"ONE, TWO, THREE, FOUR!
Now I'll need my jar," he said.

"I saw it in your room," his father said.

Caleb got the jar. He put it on the table next to the brown bag.

"That's FIVE," he said. "Let's see . . . it would be nice to take a little blanket."

"What do you think, Dad?"
Caleb's father laughed as
he worked with the bread dough.
"Good idea! Why don't you
take your blue one?"
Caleb ran to get it.
"SIX," he counted.

"Maybe Obie would like to come
with me."

"Why not?" said Dad. "Take Obie!"

Caleb called his cat and put
a black leash on him.

"SEVEN!"

"I'll put on my red coat," Caleb said.
"That will be EIGHT. And do you
think I could take your scarf, Dad?"

"It's yours!"

His father gave him a scarf
as yellow as the sun.

"NINE!" said Caleb.

Caleb looked at himself in the mirror.
"Now I have NINE things to take
with me.
ONE, TWO, THREE, FOUR, FIVE,
SIX, SEVEN, EIGHT, NINE!"

"Have everything, Caleb?"
his father called.
"Everything!" Caleb said.

He picked up the brown bag and
Obie's leash.

His father put the blue blanket
around Caleb's neck and put the jar
under his arm.

"Thanks, Dad!" Caleb said.

"You're welcome, Caleb. Have a great time!"

His father waved as Caleb and Obie went to the door.

Then Caleb stopped.

"ONE, TWO, THREE, FOUR, FIVE,
SIX, SEVEN, EIGHT, NINE — "
"Yes, Caleb?" his father asked.
He was putting the bread dough
out to rise.

"There is one more thing, Dad."
"Yes?"
"Would *you* come with me?"
"Why, Caleb! I'd love to come!"

"Then you would make TEN,
great big TEN! ONE, TWO,
THREE, FOUR, FIVE, SIX,
SEVEN, EIGHT, NINE, TEN!"

THE GREAT BIG
ENORMOUS
TURNIP

by Alexei Tolstoy

Illustrated by
Helen Oxenbury

Once upon a time an old man
planted a little turnip and said,
  "Grow, grow, little turnip,
grow sweet.
  Grow, grow, little turnip,
grow strong."
  And the turnip grew up
sweet and strong, and big
and enormous.

Then, one day, the old man
went to pull it up.

He pulled and pulled again,
but he could not pull it up.

He called the old woman.

The old woman pulled the old man.
The old man pulled the turnip.
And they pulled and pulled again,
but they could not pull it up.

So the old woman called
her granddaughter.

The granddaughter pulled the
old woman.

The old woman pulled the old man.

The old man pulled the turnip.

And they pulled and pulled again,
but they could not pull it up.

The granddaughter called
the black dog.

The black dog pulled
the granddaughter.
The granddaughter pulled
the old woman.
The old woman pulled the old man.
The old man pulled the turnip.
And they pulled and pulled again,
but they could not pull it up.

The black dog called the cat.
The cat pulled the dog.
The dog pulled the granddaughter.
The granddaughter pulled
the old woman.
The old woman pulled the old man.
The old man pulled the turnip.

And they pulled and pulled again,
but still they could not pull it up.

The cat called the mouse.

The mouse pulled the cat.

The cat pulled the dog.

The dog pulled the granddaughter.

The granddaughter pulled
the old woman.

The old woman pulled the old man.

The old man pulled the turnip.

They pulled and pulled again,
and up came the turnip at last.

The Doorbell Rang
by Pat Hutchins

Houghton Mifflin Literature

You have read some stories about
helping out. Now read one more —
The Doorbell Rang.

Find out what Grandma does to help
out when the doorbell rings and rings.

2

More and More

Doghouse for Sale

by Donna Lugg Pape

Illustrated by Derek Steele

Freckles sat and looked at his
gray doghouse.

"I need a new doghouse," he said,
"but I must sell this one first."

Freckles made a sign.

DOGHOUSE FOR SALE

Dogs came to look at Freckles'
doghouse.

But no one wanted to buy it.

"It needs to be painted,"
one dog said.

"Then I'll paint my house,"
said Freckles.

"I'll paint it red. Then someone
will buy it."

Freckles went to the store.

He got red paint and
a big paintbrush.

He worked hard. Soon the doghouse
was painted red.

"There, that looks better," he said.

Freckles made a new sign.

RED DOGHOUSE FOR SALE

Dogs came to look at Freckles'
doghouse.

But no one wanted to buy it.

One dog said, "Your house needs
a new bed."

"Then I'll make a new bed
for my doghouse," said Freckles.
"Then someone will buy it."

He went to the store to buy
what he would need.

He worked hard.

Soon the doghouse had a new bed.

Freckles made a new sign.

FOR SALE

RED DOGHOUSE WITH NEW BED

Dogs came to look at Freckles' doghouse.

But no one wanted to buy it.

One dog said, "Your house needs a window."

"Then I'll make a window for my doghouse," said Freckles. "Then someone will buy it."

He went to the store to buy a saw.

He worked hard.
Soon the doghouse had a window.
Freckles made a new sign.

FOR SALE

RED DOGHOUSE WITH NEW BED

AND A WINDOW

Dogs came to look at Freckles' house.
But no one wanted to buy it.
"Your house would look better
with some flowers in the yard,"
one dog said.

"Then I'll plant some flowers,"
said Freckles.

Freckles went to the store.

"I want to buy some flowers,"
Freckles said.

He planted the flowers
around his doghouse.

Then he made a new sign.

FOR SALE

RED DOGHOUSE WITH A NEW BED,

A WINDOW, AND FLOWERS

More dogs came to look at Freckles'
house.

"We like your house very much,"
the dogs told Freckles. "But it needs
a fence around the yard."

"A fence," said Freckles.
"That's what my house needs!"

Freckles went to the store.

"I want to buy a fence for my
doghouse," he said.

He bought a white fence.

Soon Freckles had put the fence
around his doghouse.

Then he made a new sign.

FOR SALE

RED DOGHOUSE WITH A NEW BED,

A WINDOW, FLOWERS,

AND A WHITE FENCE

Dogs came to look at the house.

"That's a fine doghouse," a dog
told Freckles.

"I want to buy it," said another.

Freckles walked around his house.

He looked at the red paint.

He looked at the window.

He looked at the pretty flowers.

He looked at the white fence.

"This is a fine doghouse,"
Freckles said. "I don't want
to sell it."

Then Freckles went inside his house
to take a nap in his new bed.

Too Much Noise

by Ann McGovern

Illustrated by Simms Taback

A long time ago there was an old
man.

His name was Peter, and he lived
in an old, old house.

The bed creaked.

The floor squeaked.

Outside, the wind blew the leaves
through the trees.
The leaves fell on the roof.
Swish. Swish.
The tea kettle whistled. *Hiss. Hiss.*
"Too noisy," said Peter.

Peter went to see the wise man
of the village.

"What can I do?" Peter asked
the wise man.

"My house makes too much noise.

My bed creaks.

My floor squeaks.

The wind blows the leaves
through the trees.

The leaves fall on the roof.
Swish. Swish.

My tea kettle whistles. *Hiss. Hiss.*"

"I can help you," the wise man said.

"I know what you can do."

"What?" said Peter.

"Get a cow," said the wise man.

"What good is a cow?" said Peter.

But Peter got a cow anyhow.

The cow said, "Moo. MOO."
The bed creaked.
The floor squeaked.
The leaves fell on the roof.
Swish. Swish.
The tea kettle whistled. *Hiss. Hiss.*

"Too noisy," said Peter.

And he went back to the wise man.

"Get a donkey," said the wise man.

"What good is a donkey?" said Peter.

But Peter got a donkey anyhow.

The donkey said, "HEE–Haw."

The cow said, "Moo. MOO."

The bed creaked.

The floor squeaked.

The leaves fell on the roof.
Swish. Swish.

The tea kettle whistled. *Hiss. Hiss.*

"Still too noisy," said Peter.

And he went back to the wise man.

"Get a sheep," said the wise man.

"What good is a sheep?" said Peter.

But Peter got a sheep anyhow.

The sheep said, "Baa. Baa."

The donkey said, "HEE-Haw."

The cow said, "Moo. MOO."

The bed creaked.

The floor squeaked.

The leaves fell on the roof.
Swish. Swish.

The tea kettle whistled. *Hiss. Hiss.*

"Too noisy," said Peter.
And he went back to the wise man.
"Get a hen," said the wise man.
"What good is a hen?" said Peter.
But Peter got a hen anyhow.

The hen said, "Cluck. Cluck."

The sheep said, "Baa. Baa."

The donkey said, "HEE–Haw."

The cow said, "Moo. MOO."

The bed creaked.

The floor squeaked.

The leaves fell on the roof.
Swish. Swish.

The tea kettle whistled. *Hiss. Hiss.*

"Too noisy," said Peter.

And back he went to the
wise man.

"Get a dog," the wise man said.
"And get a cat too."

"What good is a dog?" said Peter.
"Or a cat?"

But Peter got a dog and a cat
anyhow.

The dog said, "Woof. Woof."

The cat said, "Mee–ow. Mee–ow."

The hen said, "Cluck. Cluck."

The sheep said, "Baa. Baa."

The donkey said, "HEE–Haw."

The cow said, "Moo. MOO."

The bed creaked.

The floor squeaked.

The leaves fell on the roof.

Swish. Swish.

The tea kettle whistled. *Hiss. Hiss.*

Now Peter was angry.

He went to the wise man.

"I told you my house was too noisy," he said.

"I told you my bed creaks.

My floor squeaks.

The leaves fall on the roof.
Swish. Swish.

The tea kettle whistles.
Hiss. Hiss.

You told me to get a cow.

All day the cow says, 'Moo. MOO.'

You told me to get a donkey.

All day the donkey says,
'HEE–Haw.'

You told me to get a sheep.

All day the sheep says, 'Baa. Baa.'

You told me to get a hen.

All day the hen says, 'Cluck. Cluck.'

You told me to get a dog.

And a cat.

All day the dog says, 'Woof. Woof.'

All day the cat says, 'Mee–ow. Mee–ow.'

I am going crazy," said Peter.

The wise man said, "Do what I tell you.

Let the cow go.
Let the donkey go.
Let the sheep go.
Let the hen go.
Let the dog go.
Let the cat go."
So Peter let the cow go.

He let the donkey go.
He let the sheep go.

He let the hen go.
He let the dog go.
He let the cat go.
Now no cow said, "Moo. MOO."
No donkey said, "HEE-Haw."
No sheep said, "Baa. Baa."
No hen said, "Cluck. Cluck."
No dog said, "Woof. Woof."
No cat said, "Mee-ow. Mee-ow."

85

The bed creaked.

"Ah," said Peter. "What a quiet noise."

The floor squeaked.

"Oh," said Peter.

"What a quiet noise."

Outside the leaves fell on the roof. *Swish. Swish.*

Inside the tea kettle whistled. *Hiss. Hiss.*

"Ah. Oh," said Peter. "How quiet
my house is."

And Peter got into his bed
and went to sleep and dreamed
a very quiet dream.

I Speak

by Arnold Shapiro

Cats purr.
Lions roar.
Owls hoot.
Bears snore.
Crickets creak.
Mice squeak.
Sheep baa.
But I SPEAK!

MILLIONS OF CATS

BY WANDA GÁG

Freckles did more and more to his house. Peter got more and more animals.

In *Millions of Cats*, a little old man goes out to get a cat. Guess what he comes home with!

Solving Problems

THE WISHING WELL

A story from Mouse Tales

Written and illustrated
by Arnold Lobel

A mouse once found a wishing well.

"Now all of my wishes can come
true!" she cried.

She threw a penny into the well
and made a wish.

"OUCH!" said the wishing well.

The next day the mouse came back
to the well.

She threw a penny into the well
and made a wish.

"OUCH!" said the well.

The next day the mouse came back
again.

She threw a penny into the well.

"I wish this well would not say ouch,"
she said.

"OUCH!" said the well.

"That hurts!"

"What shall I do?" cried the mouse.
"My wishes will never come true
this way!"

The mouse ran home.
She took the pillow from her bed.
"This may help," said the mouse,
and she ran back to the well.

The mouse threw the pillow
into the well.

Then she threw a penny into the
well and made a wish.

"Ah. That feels much better!"
said the well.

"Good!" said the mouse.

"Now I can start wishing."

After that day the mouse made
many wishes by the well.

And every one of them came true.

Beatrice Doesn't Want To

from the book by Laura Joffe Numeroff

Illustrated by Heather King

Beatrice didn't like books.

She didn't even like to read.

More than that, she hated going
to the library.

But that's where her brother Henry
had to take her three days in a row.

He had to write a report on
dinosaurs.

Mother was busy and Henry had
to look after Beatrice.

"Why don't you get some books
from the shelf," Henry said when
they got to the library.

"I don't want to," Beatrice said.

"Look at how many books there are!"
Henry tried.

"I don't want to," Beatrice
said again.

"Then what do you want to do?"
Henry asked her.

"I want to watch you," she said.

"But I have to work," said Henry.

"I'll watch," Beatrice said.

"I give up," said Henry.

He worked on his report.

Beatrice watched.

Henry tried not to look at her.

The next day, Beatrice didn't even
want to go inside.

"Come on, Bea," Henry said.

"I don't want to," Beatrice told him.
"But I have to work," said Henry.
"I'll just sit outside," Beatrice said.
"OK," said Henry. "But don't move
until I come out."

Henry went inside to do his report.

All at once, he felt drops of water.
He didn't know where they were
coming from.

Then he felt someone tap him.

Henry turned around, and there was Beatrice. She was soaking wet.

"It's raining," she said.

"I give up," said Henry.

It was still raining on the last day.

Beatrice *had* to go inside this time.

She followed Henry around as he looked for more books.

"Can I hold some?" Beatrice asked.

Henry gave her some books to hold.

"They're too big," Beatrice said.

The books dropped onto her foot, and she began to cry.

"I give up!" said Henry.

"I don't know what to do with you!
Look, Bea, I've got to get this
report done. I have to take it
to school tomorrow. Please let me
work!"

"Henry," said Beatrice, "do you think
I could have a drink of water?"

And they went down a hall to look
for some water.

On the way Henry saw a poster.

This was it!

"Come on," said Henry.

"I don't want to," said Beatrice.

"That's too bad!" shouted Henry.

Soon Beatrice was in a room full of boys and girls.

Henry walked out just as she started to say "I don't want — "

"Alfred Mouse lived in a brand
new house," the librarian began
to read.

She held the book up so everyone
could see the pictures.

Beatrice just looked out the window.

"Alfred Mouse also had new roller
skates," the librarian said.

Beatrice loved to roller skate.

She looked at the librarian.

"But Alfred's mother wasn't too
happy when he skated through
the house," the librarian read.

The boys and girls laughed.

Beatrice smiled.

She remembered the time she had
tried roller skating in her own house.

Then Beatrice laughed.

She wanted to know all about
Alfred.

When the story was over, Beatrice
went up to the librarian.

"May I see that book, please?"
she asked.

"Oh, yes," said the librarian.

Beatrice sat down and looked
at the pictures over and over.

Then she felt someone tap her.

"Time to go," Henry said.

Beatrice kept looking at the pictures.

Henry stuck Beatrice's hat
on her head.

"We have to go home now," he said.

Beatrice didn't look at him.

"Come on, Bea," Henry said.

"I don't want to," Beatrice said.

Clyde Monster

From the book by Robert L. Crowe
Illustrated by Roger Pare

Clyde wasn't very old, but he
was ugly. And he was growing uglier
every day.

He lived in the woods with his parents.

Father Monster was a big, big
monster and very ugly. That was good,
because monsters will make fun of a
pretty monster.

Mother Monster was even uglier.

All in all, Clyde and his parents
were a picture family — as monsters go.

Clyde lived in a cave.

That is, he was supposed to live
in a cave, at night anyway.

During the day, he played
in the woods, doing monster things
like breathing fire.

He also did things like
turning somersaults that made
big holes in the ground, and
bumping into things.

At night, Clyde was supposed to go
to his cave and sleep.

But one night he would not
go to his cave.

"Why?" asked his mother.

"Why won't you go to your cave?"

"Because," explained Clyde, "I'm
afraid of the dark."

"Afraid?" asked his father.
"A monster of mine afraid?
 What are you afraid of?"
"People," said Clyde.
"I'm afraid there are people
in there who will get me."

"That's silly," said his father.

"Come, I'll show you."

He breathed some fire
that lit up the cave.

"There. Did you see any people?"

"No," answered Clyde.

"But they may be hiding under a rock
and they'll jump out and get me
after I'm asleep."

"That is silly," said his mother.

"There are no people here. Besides, if there were, they wouldn't hurt you."

"They wouldn't?" asked Clyde.

"No," said his mother. "Would you ever hide in the dark under a bed to scare a boy or a girl?"

"No," said Clyde, "I would never do a thing like that."

"Well, people won't hide and scare you, either," explained his father.

"A long time ago monsters and people made a deal," explained his father.

"Monsters don't scare people —
and people don't scare monsters."

"Are you sure?" Clyde asked.

"Oh, yes," said his mother.

"Do you know of a monster who
was ever scared by people?"

"No," Clyde said after thinking
it over.

"Do you know of any boys or girls
who were ever frightened
by a monster?"

"No," said Clyde.

"There!" said his mother.

"Now off to bed."

"And no more silly talk about
being scared by people,"
said his father.

"Okay," said Clyde, as he went
into the cave.

"But, could you leave the rock open
just a little?"

Night Comes

by Beatrice Schenk de Regniers

Night comes
leaking
out of the sky.
Stars come
peeking.
Moon comes
sneaking,
silvery-sly.
Who is
shaking,
shivery-
quaking?
Who is afraid
of the night?

Not I.

Chicken Little

Retold & illustrated by
STEVEN KELLOGG

❧ *Houghton Mifflin Literature* ❧

In each story you just read,
someone had a problem to solve.
Find out what happens when Chicken
Little tries to solve a problem.

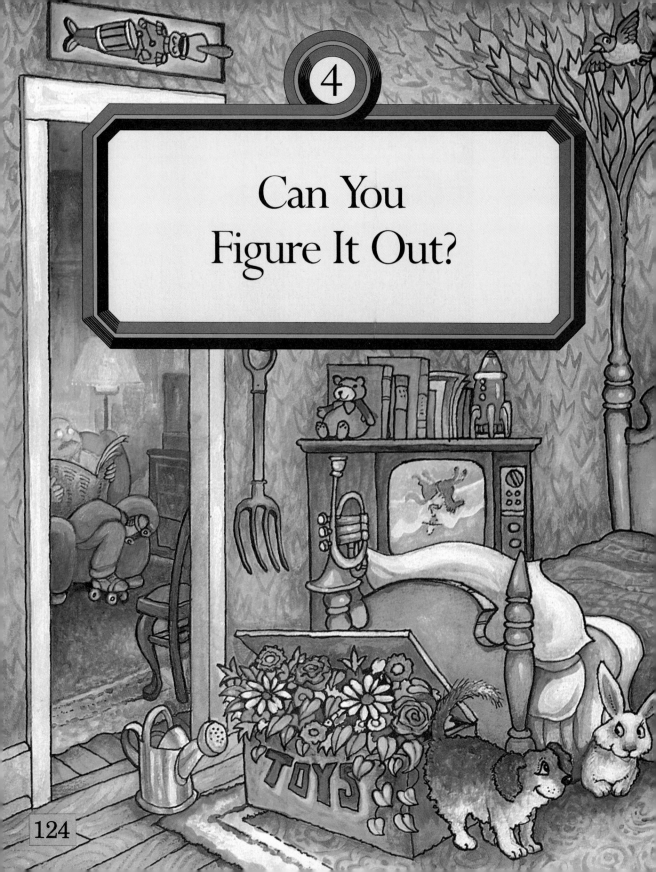

Can You Figure It Out?

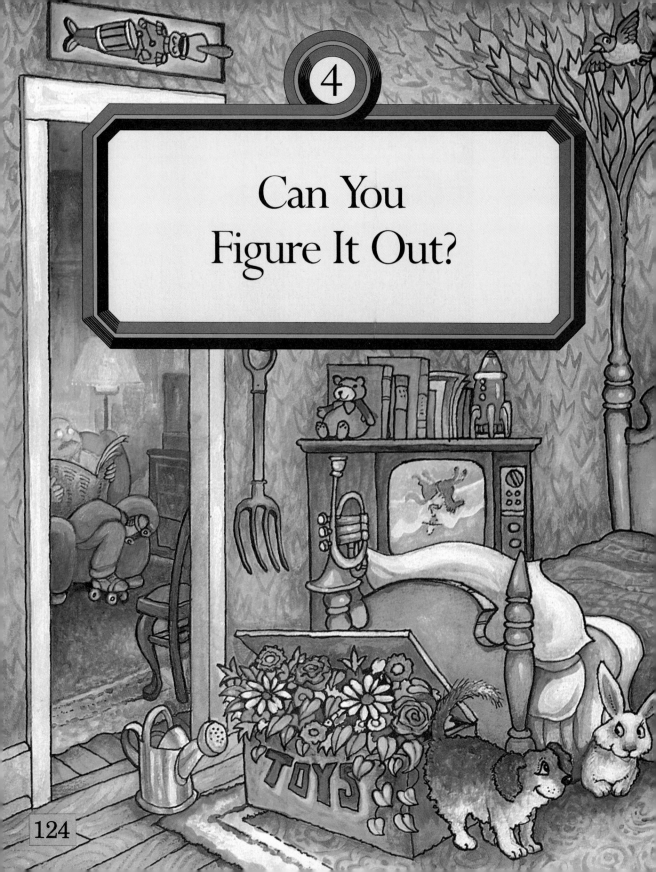

My Dog and the Key Mystery

by David A. Adler

Illustrated by Nancy Edwards Calder

My name is Jennie.

This is my dog.

My dog has four legs, brown hair, a long tail, and is real smart.

She solves mysteries.

I couldn't think of a good name for her, so I just call her My Dog.

One day, My Dog and I were sitting under a tree.

It was summer.

It was hot.

But under the tree it was cool.

My Dog poked me with her nose.

I knew what she wanted. She wanted
me to take her for a walk.

"Not now," I told her. "It's too hot."

My Dog poked me a few more times,
but I wouldn't move.

We just stayed there under the tree.

We stayed until Susan Turner
came by.

Susan was crying.

"I lost the key to my house,"
Susan said.

"My mother gave it to me this
morning.

She said I'm old enough to have
my own key.

But I lost it."

I gave Susan a tissue.

She wiped her eyes.

Then she cried some more.

My Dog poked me with her nose.

I knew what she wanted.

She wanted me to ask Susan about the key.

She wanted me to ask Susan where she had it last.

So I asked her.

"I was in front of my house when my mother gave me the key," Susan said.

"But I don't remember what I did with it."

This time I didn't wait for My Dog to poke me.

"Take us to your house," I said, "and My Dog will find the missing key."

Susan took us to her house.

We were in front of the house
when Susan told us, "I was standing
right here when my mother gave me
the key."

"But now I remember.

I didn't put the key down.

I had it in my hand when I went up
to my room."

Before we went inside, I made My
Dog wipe her feet, all four of them.

We went up to Susan's room.

It was a mess.

Toys, books, and clothing were everywhere.

It would be hard to find a key in all that mess.

I held onto My Dog.

If she got lost in that room, it would be hard to find her.

Susan stood near her bed and said, "I didn't put my key down here, either."

"I took it with me when I went into the kitchen."

Susan started to walk down to the kitchen.

My Dog poked me.

I knew what she wanted.

She wanted me to follow Susan.

I did.

The kitchen was a mess, too.

There were baking pans, mixing
bowls, and some spoons on the counter.

On the table there were cookies,
butter, and bags of sugar and flour.

Some of the flour and sugar had
spilled on the floor.

My Dog tried to help clean the
kitchen.

She licked up the spilled sugar.

"Now I remember," Susan said.

"Before I started baking the cookies, I
put the key right here."

She pointed to the counter.

I looked on the counter.

There was no key there.

Then I felt the counter.

It was sticky.

"When you baked the cookies, where did you roll out the dough?" I asked.

"Right here," Susan said.

And she pointed to the counter again.

I started to think.

I thought about the key and the dough.

While I was thinking, My Dog was climbing.

She climbed onto one of the kitchen chairs.

She was eating the cookies.

"Stop her," Susan said.

"Stop her before she eats them all."

Just then I knew what had happened to Susan's key.

"The key was on the counter when you rolled the dough.

You rolled the key up with the dough.

My Dog knows that.

She's eating your cookies to find the key."

Susan didn't think My Dog was trying to find her key.

She thought My Dog was just hungry.

Just then My Dog took a bite out of
a cookie, and a key fell out.

I picked it up and gave it to Susan.
Susan thanked me.

"Don't thank me," I said. "Thank My Dog."

Susan tried to thank My Dog.

But My Dog was busy.

There were still a few cookies left and My Dog was eating them.

Off For A Hike

by Aileen Fisher

My puppy can't speak English,
she doesn't know a letter,
but her wiggles and her wriggles
when she sees me get my sweater
and her raggle-taggle waggles
when I pack a lunch and pet her
are just as good as talking is . . .
and maybe even better.

WATCH MY TRACKS

by Bob Kaufman

illustrated by Debbie Holland

What kinds of animals visit this lake?

You can tell who they are by the tracks that they make.

Now this is a track almost everyone knows.

It's the paw of a dog. See the pad and four toes.

144

You might find these prints at the back of a house.

They're the very small prints of a shy, little mouse.

At the top of the steps is a soft shaggy mat— and tracks leading up to a hungry old cat.

145

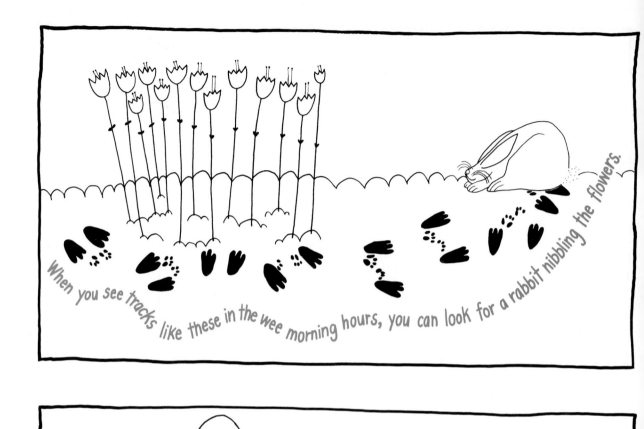

When you see tracks like these in the wee morning hours, you can look for a rabbit nibbling the flowers.

If you follow this trail by the light of the moon, near the banks of a stream you will find a raccoon.

146

Some creatures are wild and hard to get near. See the trail through the woods of a swift, timid deer.

Close to a pond you'll find web tracks like these. The swan finds webs useful for swimming with ease.

If you come to a campsite and someone's been there, you're lucky you missed him. Those are tracks of a bear.

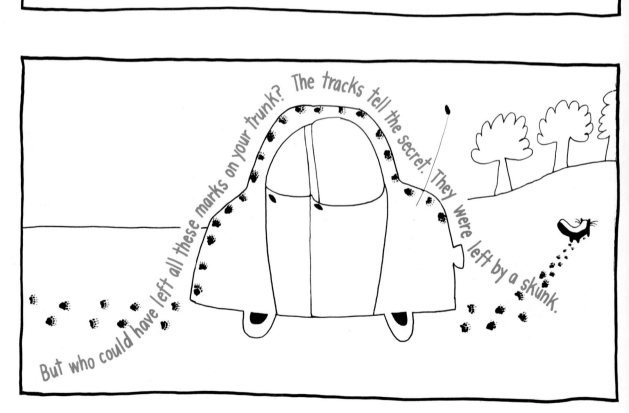

But who could have left all these marks on your trunk? The tracks tell the secret. They were left by a skunk.

148

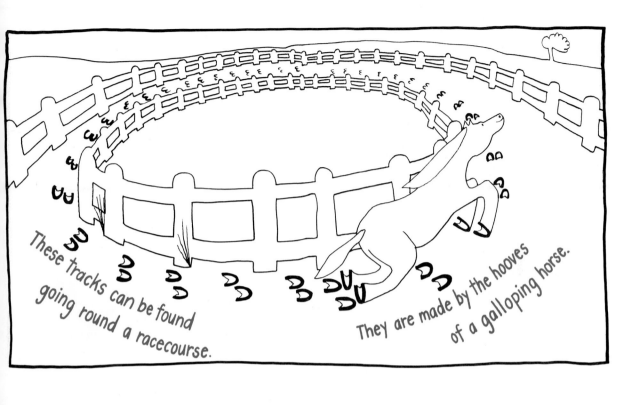

These tracks can be found going round a racecourse.

They are made by the hooves of a galloping horse.

Some tracks are little. Some tracks are big. Which belong to the bull? Which belong to the pig?

149

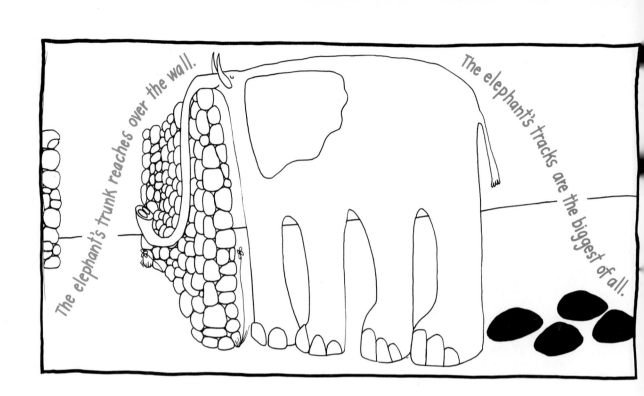

The elephant's trunk reaches over the wall.

The elephant's tracks are the biggest of all.

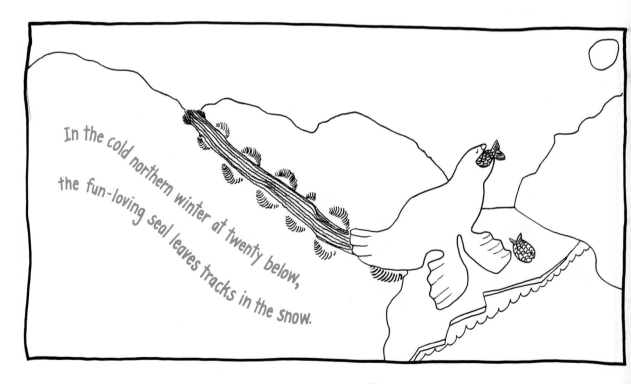

In the cold northern winter at twenty below, the fun-loving seal leaves tracks in the snow.

Leading up to a cliff on a trail high and steep are the tracks of a mountain goat. How she can leap!

And down by the shore, these marks in the sand mean a turtle is crawling from water to land.

These tracks could belong to someone you've known.

They're the footprints of people.

They might be your own.

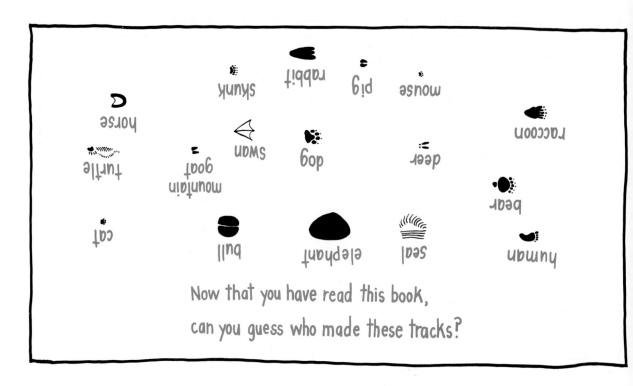

skunk rabbit pig mouse

horse raccoon

turtle mountain goat swan dog deer bear

cat bull elephant seal human

Now that you have read this book,
can you guess who made these tracks?

152

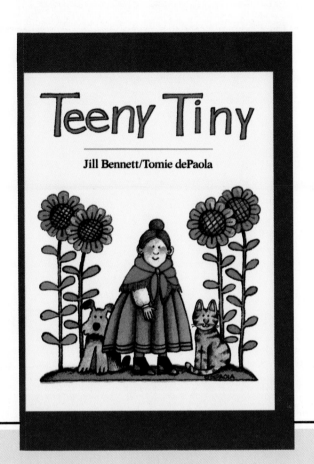

Teeny Tiny

Jill Bennett/Tomie dePaola

Houghton Mifflin Literature

Stories like *My Dog and the Key Mystery* and *Watch My Tracks* make you think a lot.

Read *Teeny Tiny*. Then read it again. Can you figure it out?

5

By
the
Pond

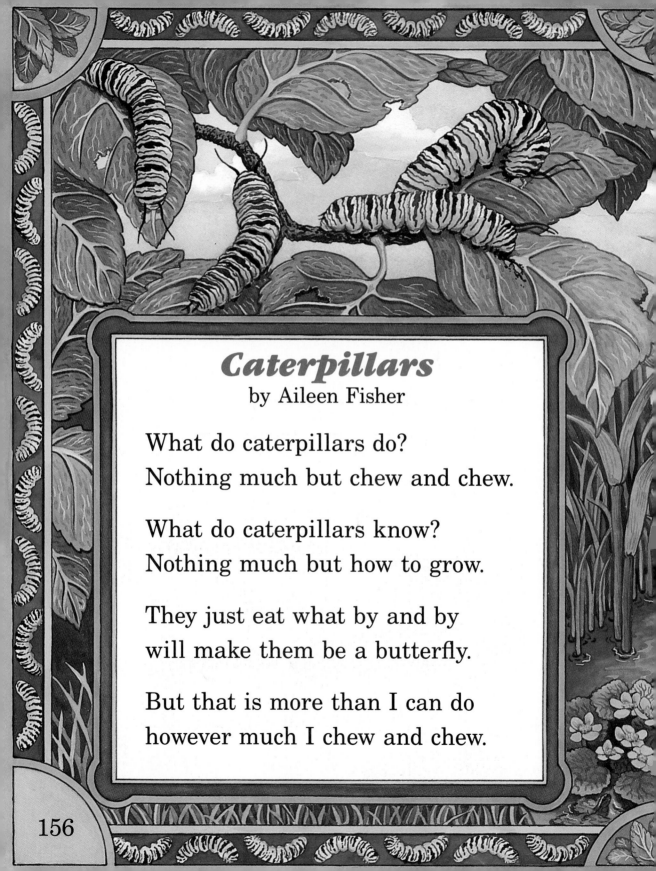

Caterpillars
by Aileen Fisher

What do caterpillars do?
Nothing much but chew and chew.

What do caterpillars know?
Nothing much but how to grow.

They just eat what by and by
will make them be a butterfly.

But that is more than I can do
however much I chew and chew.

The Polliwog
by Arthur Guiterman

Oh, the Polliwog is woggling
 In his pleasant native bog
With his beady eyes a-goggling
 Through the underwater fog
And his busy tail a-joggling
 And his eager head agog —
Just a happy little frogling
 Who is bound to be a Frog!

The
CATERPILLAR
and the
POLLIWOG

Written and Illustrated
by
JACK KENT

Caterpillars aren't like other folks.

As ducks and hippopotamuses and you and I get older, we get bigger. Especially hippopotamuses.

But not caterpillars.

They turn into butterflies.
Turning into something else like
that is not a thing just anybody can do.

Down by the pond there lived a
caterpillar who was very proud of being
different.

She bragged about it to her friends.
"When I grow up, I'm going to turn
into something else," she told the snail.

"That's nice," said the snail, who
really didn't care one way or the other.

"When I grow up, I'm going to turn into something else," she told the turtle.

"I don't blame you," said the turtle, who didn't much like wiggly things.

"When I grow up, I'm going to turn into something else," she told the polliwog.

"What fun!" said the polliwog. "What are you going to turn into?"

But the caterpillar hurried on her way, looking for someone else to tell her secret to.

"I wish *I* could turn into something else when I grow up!" said the polliwog.

"You *will*," said the fish. "*All* polliwogs do."

"What am I going to turn into?" the polliwog asked.

But the fish saw a tasty bug and dashed after it.

"When I grow up," said the
caterpillar, who had circled the pond
and was going around for the second
time, "when I grow up," she told the
polliwog again, "I'm going to turn into
something else."

"So am *I*!" said the polliwog.

"*You*?!" The caterpillar was so surprised she almost fell into the pond.

"The fish said so," the polliwog told her. "Fish know things. They go to school."

The caterpillar was upset.

"I thought only caterpillars could do it," she said rather sadly.

"What are we going to turn into?" the polliwog asked.

"Well, *I'm* going to turn into a
butterfly!" said the caterpillar.

"Then I guess I will, too!" the
polliwog said happily. "What fun! Let's
do it together!"

"All right," the caterpillar agreed, although she would rather have done it alone. "But I get to go first!"

The polliwog didn't mind. He wasn't at all sure how it was done. "I'll watch you," he said.

So when the time came, the
caterpillar started to spin a cocoon.

"This is the tricky part," she said.

The polliwog watched as the
caterpillar spun.

Soon only her head was uncovered.

"Now I have to close the lid," she said. "And when I come out, I'll be a butterfly."

"Go ahead!" the polliwog said excitedly. "I want to see you do it!"

"It will take a while," the caterpillar warned. She started spinning again and was soon out of sight in the cocoon.

For a long time nothing happened.
But the polliwog was patient.

He watched and watched and
watched, for days and days and days.

At last there was activity in the cocoon.

The end of it opened and, very slowly, the caterpillar climbed out.

Only she wasn't a caterpillar anymore.

She was a *butterfly*. A beautiful yellow butterfly.

The polliwog was so excited he hopped up and down with delight!

He *hopped*! Up and down! Like a *frog*!

"I was so busy watching *you*," he said, "I didn't notice what was happening to *me*!"

"You're a very handsome frog," the butterfly said, as she flew off to try her new wings.

But the frog was puzzled.

"I thought I was going to be a butterfly," he said.

A caterpillar wiggled by.

"When I grow up," he said proudly to the frog, "I'm going to turn into something else!"

But the frog wasn't listening.

He was admiring his reflection in
the water.

"I *am*, you know, a *very* handsome
frog!" he said.

The Hungry Fox
and the Foxy Duck

by **Kathleen Leverich**

Illustrated by Gavin Bishop

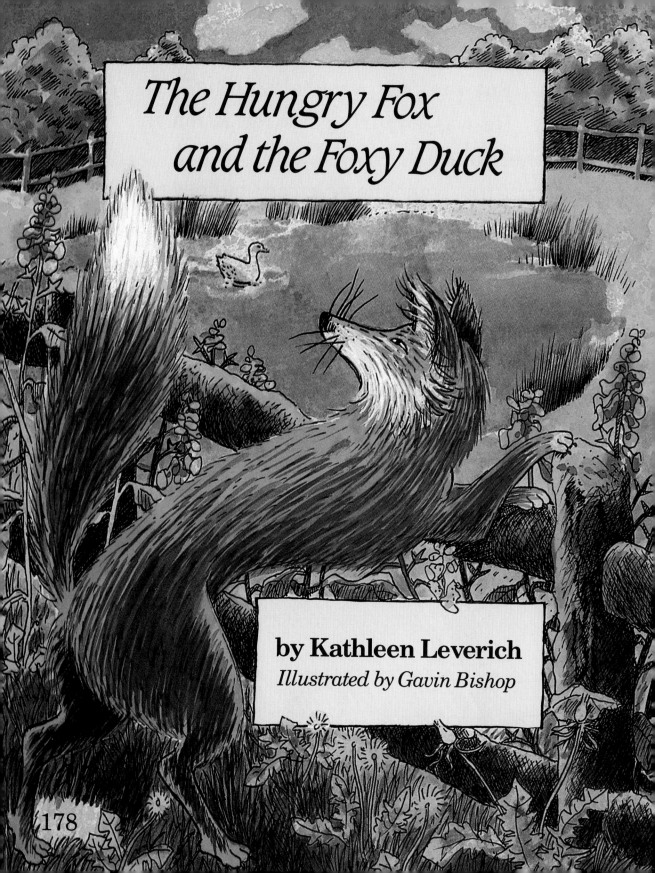

Not far from here there once lived a very wise little duck.

This little duck lived on a pond in a field with a fence all around.

All day long, the little duck would sun herself and swim.

Life was peaceful on the pond in the field with the fence all around.

One morning the little duck saw a hungry red fox. The fox stood on the bank of the pond.

"Come and have breakfast with me," Fox called to Duck.

Duck looked at Fox.

"This fox is hungry," she thought to herself. "He looks hungry for ducks."

The little duck thought quickly.

"How can we eat breakfast without a table?" she asked.

"Wait right there," called Fox. "I will get a table."

Fox ran across the field.

He ran over the fence.

He ran through the forest until he
came to a woodcutter's hut.

Fox looked inside.

No one was home, but a little table
stood by the window.

"Woodcutter won't miss this table,"
thought Fox.

And he stole the table.

Back ran the fox to the pond in the field with the fence all around.

Fox could almost smell the roast duck he would have for supper.

The little duck was swimming in the middle of the pond.

"Here is a table," called Fox. "Come and have breakfast with me, Duck."

"You are too late," called the little duck. "I ate while you were gone. Now it is almost lunch time."

"Well then," called Fox. "Come have lunch with me."

Fox was very hungry for roast duck after all that running.

The little duck thought quickly.

"How can we eat lunch without plates and cups?" she asked.

"Wait right there," called Fox. "I will get plates and cups."

Fox ran across the field.

He ran under the fence.

He ran down the road until he came
to a potter's shed.

The potter was not there, but Fox
saw a pile of plates and cups.

"Potter will not miss these,"
thought Fox.

And he stole two plates and
two cups.

Back ran the fox to the pond in the field with the fence all around.

Fox could almost taste the roast duck he would have for supper.

The little duck was swimming in the middle of the pond.

"Here are the plates and cups," called Fox. "Come have lunch with me, Duck."

"You are too late," called the little duck. "I ate while you were gone. Now it is almost supper time."

"It is indeed," said Fox, and he licked his chops. "Come have supper with me."

Fox was tired and cranky and hungry for roast duck after all that running.

The little duck thought quickly.

"How can we eat without a tablecloth?" she asked.

"If I get a tablecloth, *then* will you eat supper with me?" demanded Fox.

"Yes," said the little duck.

"Wait right there," called Fox. "I will get a tablecloth."

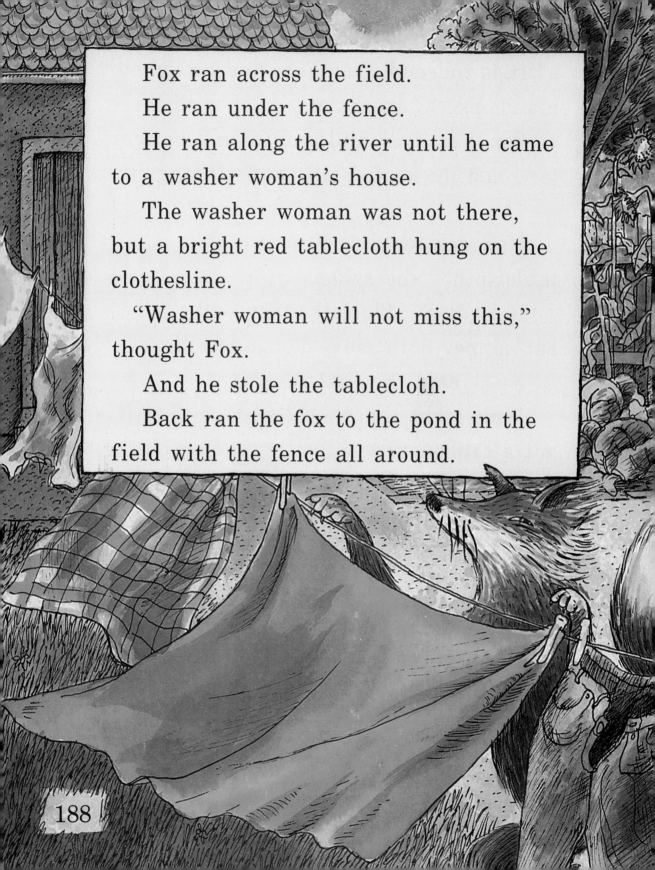

Fox ran across the field.

He ran under the fence.

He ran along the river until he came to a washer woman's house.

The washer woman was not there, but a bright red tablecloth hung on the clothesline.

"Washer woman will not miss this," thought Fox.

And he stole the tablecloth.

Back ran the fox to the pond in the field with the fence all around.

Fox could hardly wait for the first
bite of his roast duck supper.

The little duck was swimming in the
middle of the pond.

"Here is a tablecloth," called Fox.
"Come for supper, Duck."

"Hold up the tablecloth, Fox," called
the wise little duck. "I do not think it
is big enough."

"It is big enough," called Fox.

And he waved the red tablecloth to
prove it.

Then Fox learned why the field had a fence all around it.

Fox never came back.

Duck lived happily.

Life was peaceful on the pond in the field with the fence all around to keep the bull in.

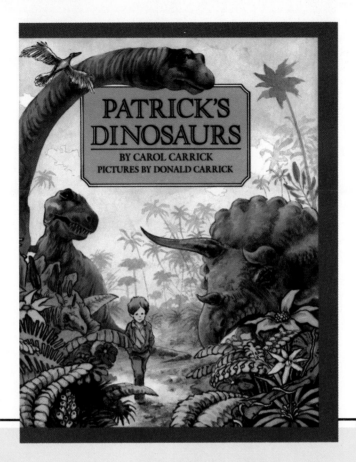

PATRICK'S
DINOSAURS
BY CAROL CARRICK
PICTURES BY DONALD CARRICK

❧ Houghton Mifflin Literature ❧

You may have seen a caterpillar,
a polliwog, or a duck by a pond. But
have you ever seen a dinosaur?

You may <u>think</u> you see one after
you read *Patrick's Dinosaurs*.

6

Old Friends,
New Friends

We Are
Best Friends

Written and illustrated

by Aliki

Peter came to tell Robert the news.

"I am moving away," he said.

"You can't move away," said Robert. "We are best friends."

"I am moving far away," said Peter.

"What will you do without me?" asked Robert. "Who will you play with?"

"We will live in a new house," said Peter.

"You will miss my birthday party!" said Robert.

"I will be going to a new school," said Peter.

"Who will you fight with?" asked Robert. "Nobody fights like best friends."

"I will make new friends," said Peter.

"You can't move away," said Robert.
"You will miss me too much."

But Peter moved away.

There was nothing to do without
Peter.

There was no one to play with.

There was no one to share with.

There was no one to fight with. Not the way best friends fight.

There was no fun anymore.

"I'll bet Peter doesn't even remember me," said Robert. "It's a good thing he's not here. I'd have to punch him one."

"Hello. My name is Will," said a new face.

I don't like freckles, thought Robert.

"I used to go to another school," said Will.

I don't like glasses, thought Robert.

"My friends are all there," said Will.

I don't like silly names like Will, thought Robert.

"It was fun," said Will. "Not boring like this place."

A letter came for Robert. A letter from Peter.

DEAR ROBERT,

I HOPE YOU STILL REMEMBER ME.

I LIKE MY NEW HOUSE NOW.

I LIKE MY NEW SCHOOL NOW.

AT FIRST I DIDN'T LIKE ANYTHING. BUT NOW I HAVE A FRIEND, ALEX. YOU ARE MY BEST FRIEND, BUT ALEX IS NICE.

IT IS FUN TO HAVE SOMEONE TO PLAY WITH AGAIN.

IT'S NOT SO LONELY.

LOVE,
PETER

Robert drew Peter a letter.

He drew two friends building a fort.

He drew them playing with their cars.

He drew them riding their bikes.

He wrote:

IF YOU WERE HERE, THIS IS WHAT WE'D BE DOING. BUT YOU'RE NOT.

Then he wrote:

THERE IS A NEW BOY IN SCHOOL. HE HAS FRECKLES.

Robert saw Will by the fence.

"Did you lose something?" he asked.

"I thought I saw a frog," said Will.

"That's funny, looking for a frog,"
said Robert.

"What's funny about it? I like frogs,"
said Will.

"I used to have a pet frog named
Greenie. He'd wait for me by the pond
near where I lived. He must miss me a
lot."

"I know where there are frogs," said Robert. "Right in my garden."

"You're just saying that," said Will.

"I mean it," said Robert. "You can see for yourself."

"If I had a frog in my garden, I'd share it," said Will.

"That's what I'm doing," said Robert.

Robert and Will rode home together.
They went straight into the garden.
The frogs were there.

One leaped under a bush, and Will
caught it.

"I'll call you Greenie the Second," he
said. "You like me already, don't you?"

"The frogs lay their eggs here every
year," said Robert. "It's almost time.

My friend Peter used to come watch
the tadpoles. He called them
Inkywiggles. He'll miss them."

"Why?" asked Will.

"He moved away," said Robert. "Just about the time you came. I write him letters."

"Then you can write about the Inkywiggles," said Will.

They laughed.

"I haven't had so much fun since I moved here," said Will.

"Neither have I," said Robert.

Robert wrote to Peter.

DEAR PETER,

I CAN'T WAIT UNTIL SUMMER
WHEN YOU COME TO VISIT.

THE NEW BOY IS CALLED WILL.

I SHOWED HIM THE FROGS.

HE HAD A PET ONE NEAR HIS
HOME.

BUT HE HAD TO MOVE AWAY,
LIKE YOU.

HE THINKS INKYWIGGLES IS
FUNNY.

I'LL WRITE WHEN THEY HATCH.

LOVE, ROBERT.

P.S. HOW IS ALEX?

P.P.S. SEE YOU SOON.

Robert mailed the letter, then rode
over to Will's house to play.

The Morning Walk
by A. A. Milne

When Anne and I go out a walk,
We hold each other's hand and talk
Of all the things we mean to do
When Anne and I are forty-two.

And when we've thought about a thing,
Like bowling hoops or bicycling,
Or falling down on Anne's balloon,
We do it in the afternoon.

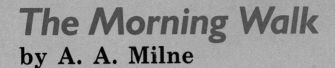

Harriet and the Garden

by Nancy Carlson

Illustrated by Cathie Bleck

It was a beautiful summer day.

Harriet was playing ball with some pals.

Across the park, Mrs. Hoozit was working in her garden.

Mrs. Hoozit had been waiting for
this day for a long time.

Her prize dahlia was in full bloom.

"I must call the garden club and have
them come over today and have a look,"
she said.

Meanwhile, Harriet was playing
outfield.

Suddenly George hit a fly ball.

Harriet just had to catch it.

If she didn't, it would be a home run for sure.

Harriet ran back and back.

She kept her eyes on the ball.

She was concentrating so hard that she never even noticed when she came to Mrs. Hoozit's garden.

She ran backward right through the perfect mums.

Then she trampled through the lilies.

In the middle of the rose bushes she caught the ball.

And then she fell down right on top of the prize dahlia in full bloom.

"Oops," said Harriet.

"Let's get out of here," said her pals.

Everyone ran except for Harriet.

She looked around her at the garden.

Everything was ruined.

Suddenly Harriet heard Mrs. Hoozit's voice. "What's happened to my beautiful garden?"

Harriet was so scared that she just took off.

She ran and she ran and she never turned back.

Harriet ran all the way home, up the stairs, and into her bedroom.

She slammed the door.

Maybe she didn't recognize me, thought Harriet.

"Are you all right, Harriet?" Mother asked.

"Just fine," said Harriet.

But she decided she'd better spend the rest of the day inside.

That night Harriet couldn't eat her supper.

She didn't even care when Mother made popcorn balls.

Her favorite television program wasn't very interesting.

When Harriet went to bed, she couldn't sleep.

And when she finally fell asleep, she had bad dreams.

The next morning Harriet made a decision.

She went straight to Mrs. Hoozit's house and confessed.

Then she spent the rest of the day helping Mrs. Hoozit plant new flowers and tie up the broken rose bushes.

They had a good time.

When Harriet got home, she was a
mess.

"Harriet, are you all right?" Mother
asked.

"Just fine!" said Harriet.

Ira
Sleeps
Over

Written and
illustrated
by Bernard Waber

I was invited to sleep at Reggie's house.

Was I happy!

I had never slept at a friend's house before.

But I had a problem.

It began when my sister said:

"Are you taking your teddy bear along?"

"Taking my teddy bear along!" I said.
"To my friend's house? Are you
kidding?

That's the silliest thing I ever heard!

Of course, I'm not taking my teddy
bear."

And then she said:

"But you never slept without your
teddy bear before.

How will you feel sleeping without
your teddy bear for the very first time?
Hmmmmmmm?"

"I'll feel fine.

I'll feel great.

I will probably love sleeping without my teddy bear.

Just don't worry about it," I said.

"Who's worried?" she said.

But now, she had me thinking about it.

Now, she really had me thinking about it.

I began to wonder:

Suppose I won't like sleeping without my teddy bear.

Suppose I just hate sleeping without my teddy bear.

Should I take him?

"Take him," said my mother.

"Take him," said my father.

"But Reggie will laugh," I said. "He'll say I'm a baby."

"He won't laugh," said my mother.

"He won't laugh," said my father.

"He'll laugh," said my sister.

I decided not to take my teddy bear.

That afternoon, I played with Reggie. Reggie had plans, big plans.

"Tonight," he said, "when you come to my house, we are going to have fun, fun, fun.

First, I'll show you my junk collection.

And after that we'll have a wrestling match.

And after that, a pillow fight.

And after that we'll do magic tricks.

And after that we'll play checkers.

And after that we'll play dominoes.

And after that we can fool around with my magnifying glass."

"Great!" I said. "I can hardly wait."

"By the way," I asked, "what do you think of teddy bears?"

But Reggie just went on talking and planning as if he had never heard of teddy bears.

"And after that," he said, "do you know what we can do after that — I mean when the lights are out and the house is really dark? Guess what we can do?"

"What?" I asked.

"We can tell ghost stories."

"Ghost stories?" I said.

"Ghost stories," said Reggie, "scary, creepy, spooky ghost stories."

I began to think about my teddy bear.

"Does your house get very dark?" I asked.

"Uh-huh," said Reggie.

"Very, very dark?"

"Uh-huh," said Reggie.

"By the way," I said again, "what do you think of teddy bears?"

Suddenly, Reggie was in a big hurry to go someplace.

"See you tonight," he said.

"See you," I said.

I decided to take my teddy bear.

"Good," said my mother.

"Good," said my father.

But my sister said:

"What if Reggie wants to know your teddy bear's name. Did you think about that?

And did you think about how he will laugh and say Tah Tah is a silly, baby name, even for a teddy bear?"

"He won't ask," I said.

"He'll ask," she said.

I decided not to take my teddy bear.

At last, it was time to go to Reggie's house.

"Good night," said my mother.

"Good night," said my father.

"Sleep tight," said my sister.

I went next door where Reggie lived.

That night, Reggie showed me his junk.

He showed me his flashlight, his collection of bottle caps, a chain made of chewing gum wrappers, some picture postcards, an egg timer, jumbo goggles, a false nose and mustache, and a bunch of old rubber stamps and labels from his father's office.

We decided to play "office" with the rubber stamps.

After that we had a wrestling match.

And after that we had a pillow fight.

And after that Reggie's father said:

"Bedtime!"

"Already?" said Reggie.

"Already," said his father.

We got into bed.

"Good night," said Reggie's father.

"Good night," we said.

Reggie sighed.

I sighed.

"We can still tell ghost stories," said
Reggie.

"Do you know any?" I asked.

"Uh-huh," said Reggie.

Reggie began to tell a ghost story:

"Once there was this ghost and he
lived in a haunted house only he did
most of the haunting himself.

This house was empty except for this
ghost because nobody wanted to go near
this house, they were so afraid of this
ghost.

And every night this ghost would walk around this house and make all kinds of clunky, creeky sounds. *Aroomp! Aroomp!* Like that.

And he would go around looking for people to scare because that's what he liked most to do: scare people.

And he was very scary to look at.

Oh, was he scary to look at!"

Reggie stopped.

"Are you scared?" he asked.

"Uh-huh," I said. "Are you?"

"What?" said Reggie.

"Are you scared?"

"Just a minute," said Reggie, "I have to get something."

"What do you have to get?" I asked.

"Oh, something," said Reggie.

Reggie pulled the something out of a drawer.

The room was dark, but I could see it had fuzzy arms and legs and was about the size of a teddy bear.

I looked again.

It was a teddy bear.

Reggie got back into bed.

"Now, about this ghost . . ." he said.

"Is that your teddy bear?" I asked.

"What?" said Reggie.

"Is that your teddy bear?"

"You mean this teddy bear?"

"The one you're holding," I said.

"Uh-huh," Reggie answered.

"Do you sleep with him all of the time?"

"What?" said Reggie.

"Do you sleep with him all of the time?"

"Uh-huh."

"Does your teddy bear have a name? Does your teddy bear have a name?" I said louder.

"Uh-huh," Reggie answered.

"What is it?"

"You won't laugh?" said Reggie.

"No, I won't laugh," I said.

"Promise?"

"I promise."

"It's Foo Foo."

"Did you say 'Foo Foo'?"

"Uh-huh," said Reggie.

"Just a minute," I said, "I have to get something."

"What do you have to get?" Reggie asked.

"Oh, something," I answered.

The next minute, I was ringing my own doorbell.

The door opened.

"Ira!" everyone said.

"What are you doing here?"

"I changed my mind," I answered.

"You what!" said my mother.

"You what!" said my father.

"You what!" said my sister. (She was still up.)

"I changed my mind," I said. "I decided to take Tah Tah after all."

I went upstairs.

Soon, I was down again with Tah Tah.

My sister said:

"Reggie will laugh.

You'll see how he'll laugh.

He's just going to fall down laughing."

"He won't laugh," said my mother.

"He won't laugh," said my father.

"He won't laugh," I said.

I came back to Reggie's room.

"I have a teddy bear, too," I said. "Do you want to know his name?"

I waited for Reggie to say, Uh-huh.

But Reggie didn't say, Uh-huh.

Reggie didn't say anything.

I looked at Reggie.

He was fast asleep. Just like that,
he had fallen asleep.

"Reggie! Wake up!" I said. "You have
to finish telling the ghost story."

But Reggie just held his teddy bear
closer and went right on sleeping.

And after that — well, there wasn't
anything to do after that.

"Good night," I whispered to Tah Tah.

And I fell asleep, too.

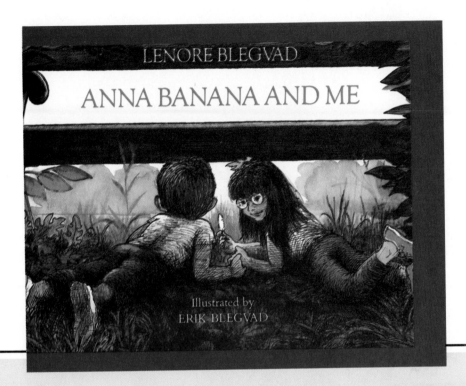

LENORE BLEGVAD

ANNA BANANA AND ME

Illustrated by
ERIK BLEGVAD

Houghton Mifflin Literature

Here is another story about friends
— *Anna Banana and Me.*

Read what a boy and his friend, Anna
Banana, like to see and do together.

Something Special

7

Willaby

**Written and illustrated by
Rachel Isadora**

Willaby is in first grade.

She likes math, lunch, her teacher
Miss Finney, and science.

But best of all Willaby likes to draw.

When the other children are playing,
Willaby is drawing.

She draws on her desk when all the
others write the history lesson in their
notebooks.

At home Willaby sometimes uses up
all her paper.

Then she draws on the walls in her
bedroom.

One Monday morning when Willaby goes to school, Miss Finney is not there.

The substitute teacher, Mrs. Benjamin, tells the class that Miss Finney is sick and will not come back to school until the following Monday.

The class decides to send Miss
Finney get-well cards.

They make up a poem and Mrs.
Benjamin writes it on the blackboard.

Soon everyone is busy copying the
poem. Except for Willaby.

She is busy drawing a fire truck she
saw on her way to school.

Before long Mrs. Benjamin asks the class to hand in their cards.

Willaby doesn't know what to do.

She forgot all about the get-well card and now there is no time to copy the poem.

The children put their cards in a big envelope.

On the way home from school,
Willaby suddenly remembers she didn't
sign her name on her card!

Now Miss Finney will never know
that she sent her a card.

Miss Finney might think she doesn't
like her.

During the week Willaby makes
thirty-seven get-well cards for Miss
Finney. She signs every one.

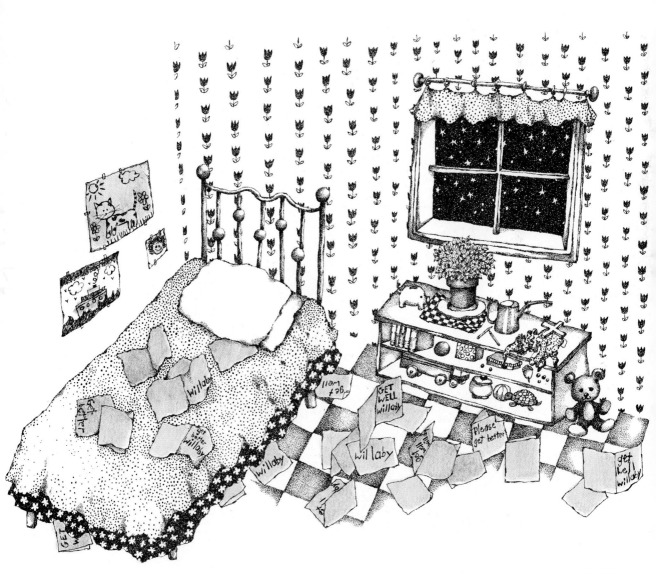

But when Monday morning comes,
Willaby does not feel like going to
school.

Instead of taking the bus, she
decides to walk to school.

Willaby walks to her seat without
looking at Miss Finney.

But when she sits down at her
desk. . . .

Dear Willaby,
Thank you for
the get-well
picture.

Miss Finney

Willaby doesn't give Miss Finney the
thirty-seven get-well cards.

She doesn't have to!

GOOD AS NEW

by Barbara Douglass

Illustrated by Patience Brewster

I thought my Grandpa could fix anything.

One morning last week he fixed the hose and the fence, and my swing and my sandbox, and Yim Lee's fire engine, and Carmen's wagon.

But then my cousin K.C. came to visit while Uncle Jonathan went riding with his club.

And K.C. started crying as soon as my uncle rode away.

Nobody could make him happy, not even Grandpa.

Because the only thing K.C. wanted was my bear.

And I said, "Huh-uh. Nobody plays with my bear but me."

K.C. kicked the floor and he cried some more and Mom said, "Grady, do you think K.C. feels lonely because he didn't bring *his* bear?"

Then Dad said, "Do you think he might feel better, son, if you just let him hold your bear?"

Grandpa didn't say anything, and K.C. cried even harder until Yim Lee and Carmen grabbed their toys and went home.

Grandpa grabbed his hat and went for a walk.

And before I could say, "Okay, you can HOLD him," K.C. grabbed my bear.

But he didn't just hold him.

He dragged my bear around by the ears, and he fed him peanut butter, and he tried to feed him to the dog.

Dad made him stop.

Then K.C. dragged my bear outside where he sat on him, and he turned the hose on him.

Dad made him stop that, too.

So K.C. buried my bear in the sand.

After K.C. went home, I dug up
my bear.

Mom said, "Please, don't bring it in
the house."

Dad said, "I'm sorry it's ruined, son,
but I'll buy you a new one."

I said, "I don't want a new bear. I
want this old one fixed the way he was
before K.C. came."

Mom shook her head and Dad did, too.

But Grandpa hung up his hat and he said, "Never you mind now, Grady. I can fix that bear so he'll be as good as new in no time."

Then he brought a big brown paper bag outside and we sat down.

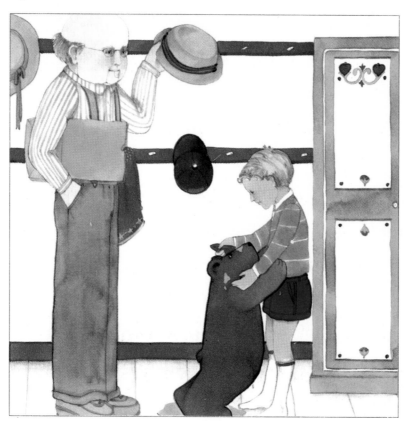

But he opened up his pocket knife!

I said, "*Wait* a minute. What's that for, Grandpa? Are you sure you can fix my bear?"

"Of course I can," he said to me. "Hold on here and pull so I can see to cut the stitches."

I held on and I pulled, but I didn't
want to watch.

Because Grandpa opened up my
bear — and then — he started pulling out
the stuffing!

My bear's stomach went flat, the
way mine feels when I'm hungry.

His arms and legs wrinkled up, too,
so I said, "Grandpa, are you sure this
is the right way to fix my bear?"

Grandpa just kept on working.

My bear's nose dropped and his head flopped, and I covered up my eyes and I said, "Grandpa! Are you sure?"

But he said, "Never you mind now, Grady. We'll have this bear as good as new in no time."

In the kitchen we made a sinkful of suds and Grandpa scrubbed my bear.

First he scrubbed the stomach, and then the arms and legs, and the neck and the nose, and he even scrubbed the ears.

The water got all muddy but my
bear didn't get very clean.

"Look," I said to Grandpa. "I can still
see peanut butter."

So I pulled the plug and we made
more suds, and Grandpa scrubbed
again.

But this time he scrubbed too hard.

Both the ears fell off and I said,
"Grandpa! I'm not sure this is the right
way to fix my bear."

"Never you mind, now," Grandpa
said. "He'll be as good as new in no
time."

Grandpa rinsed my bear and squeezed him hard, but when he shook him out, I told him, "Grandpa, a clean bear's not so good if it's all flat and wrinkled and it hasn't got any ears!"

"Never you mind, now," Grandpa said.

Then he hung my bear outside to dry, with one ear on each side, and he said, "I have to go downtown to buy new stuffing. Anybody want to come along?"

I did.

We rode the bus to the hobby shop.

While Grandpa bought the stuffing, I saved his place in the popcorn line.

By the time we got back home again,
my bear and his ears were dry.
But he was still all flat and broken.
I said, "Grandpa? Are you sure . . ."
I guess you know what Grandpa said.

So we sat down outside again.

And Grandpa filled my bear with new fluffy stuffing.

He put about a hundred hunks of stuffing in the arms, and he put about a hundred hunks of stuffing in the legs, and he put about a hundred hunks of stuffing in the head, and in the nose, and in the neck.

But the stomach still looked hungry.

So Grandpa kept on stuffing.

Then I brought him a needle and
thread and a thimble, and he sewed the
back of my bear and said, "There. . . ."

But I said, "Wait a minute, Grandpa!
He isn't dirty anymore and he isn't flat
or wrinkled, but he still doesn't look so
good without . . ."

"Without what? Is something
missing?" my grandpa asked, wide-eyed.

"Never you mind," he said. "I can fix that, too."

So he did. And then he said, "There now, how does that look?"

I turned my bear all around and carefully looked it over.

"Grandpa," I said at last, "I thought you could fix anything. But this bear isn't good as new."

There was a long silence and
Grandpa looked kind of sad.

"It's *better* than new!" I shouted,
laughing. And I gave him my best
bear hug.

Now whenever K.C. comes to visit, Grandpa and I grab our hats (and my bear) and slip out the back door, neverminding.

My Teddy Bear

by Marchette Chute

A teddy bear is a faithful friend.
You can pick him up at either end.
His fur is the color
  of breakfast toast,
And he's always there
  when you need him most.

Two Good Friends

by **Judy Delton**
Illustrated by
Giulio Maestro

Duck had cleaned his house.
All his floors were waxed.
All his furniture was polished.
He was admiring his clean rooms
when he heard a knock at the door.

It was Bear.

"Come in," said Duck, "but first wipe
your feet on the mat."

Bear wiped his feet on the mat and
went inside.

"Make yourself at home," said Duck.
"Thank you, I will," said Bear, and
he sat down in a shiny rocking chair.
Then he put his feet on Duck's table.
Duck reached for a newspaper and
put it under Bear's feet.

"What do you have to eat?" asked
Bear.

"Nothing," said Duck.

"Nothing?" asked Bear.

"Today I cleaned my house,"
explained Duck. "I did not bake."

"Well, I have something," said Bear, and he reached into his pocket and took out two brownies.

"Bear," said Duck, "you are spilling crumbs on my floor," and he reached for another newspaper and put it under Bear's chair.

Bear looked at the newspaper. Then
he looked at the two brownies.

"Duck," he said, "you are a very good
housekeeper, but what good is a clean
house if you have nothing to eat? Here,
have a brownie."

Bear and Duck each ate a brownie
and spent the rest of the afternoon
putting a puzzle together.

The next day Duck went to visit
Bear.

"Duck!" said Bear. "How nice to see
you. Come right in."

"M-m-m-m," said Duck. "What smells
so good?"

"I've been baking," said Bear, and he pointed to two honey cakes and two nut pies sitting on the table. "Brush the flour off a chair and sit down."

"Bear," said Duck. "I can't sit down. My feet are stuck."

"Oh dear," said Bear. "That's the honey."

"Would you like honey cake or nut pie?" he asked.

"Nut pie," said Duck, who had finally managed to unstick his feet. "I've had enough honey for one day."

"O.K.," said Bear, and he cut one piece of nut pie for Duck and one for himself.

"May I have a plate?" asked Duck.

"The plates are dirty," said Bear.

"Well, then, may I have a fork?"
asked Duck.

"The forks are dirty too," said Bear.
He looked ashamed.

"Bear," said Duck, "how do you expect me to eat?"

"I'm sorry," said Bear, "but today I baked. I didn't clean the house or wash the dishes. Maybe you can use your wings. The pie will still taste good."

Duck and Bear each ate a piece of pie.

When Duck finished, he licked the
tips of his wings. "I must say, Bear,
you are a terrible housekeeper but your
nut pie is the best I have ever tasted."

Bear smiled. "Have another piece,"
he said.

"Gladly," said Duck, and they each
ate another piece.

The next day Bear went to Duck's
house with a surprise.

Duck was not at home but Bear went
inside anyway.

He put six raspberry muffins on the
table and wrote a note. "From Bear," it
said. Then he went home.

When Bear walked into his house, he was surprised.

"I must be in the wrong house," he thought.

His feet did not stick to the floor.

The dishes were washed and on the shelf.

He did not see his name where he had written it in the flour on the table.

Instead he saw a note: "From Duck."

"I must thank Duck," thought Bear,
but just then there was a knock on the
door.

It was Duck.

"Thank you for the muffins," said
Duck. "I was so surprised. And it's not
even my birthday."

"And I have never seen my house so clean," said Bear. "I was surprised too."

"We really are good friends," said Duck.

"Yes!" cried Bear. "Let's celebrate! Come in and have some cookies."

"But first," added Bear, "wipe your feet on the mat."

"Of course," said Duck. And he did.

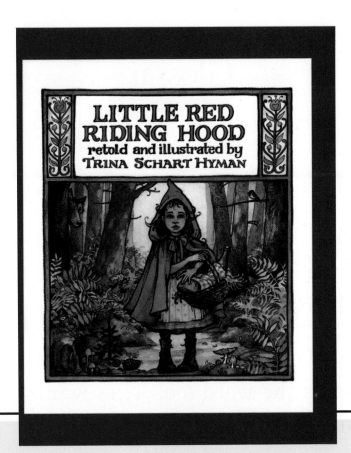

Houghton Mifflin Literature

You have read about characters who did something special. Little Red Riding Hood takes something special to Grandma. Find out what happens when she meets a hungry wolf!

Glossary

A

again To do something <u>again</u> means to do it one more time: I like this book, so I will read it <u>again</u>.

also The word <u>also</u> means about the same as the word *too*: Tina wants to play, and I do <u>also</u>.

B

bank **1.** You put money in a <u>bank</u>. **2.** A <u>bank</u> can also be the ground beside a river: We like to sit on the river <u>bank</u>.

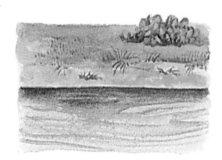

beautiful   Something <u>beautiful</u> is very pretty: It is a <u>beautiful</u> morning.

build   To <u>build</u> means to make something: I am <u>building</u> a playhouse.

bury   To <u>bury</u> something means to cover it up: The dog <u>buried</u> a bone.

buy   When you <u>buy</u> something, you pay money for it: We went to the pet store to <u>buy</u> a fish.

C

celebrate   To <u>celebrate</u> means to have fun at a special time: Let's <u>celebrate</u> your birthday with a cake.

climb   To <u>climb</u> means to go up:
The cat is <u>climbing</u> up the tree.

count   When you <u>count</u>, you find
out how many things there are:
Can you <u>count</u> the books?

cry   **1.** To <u>cry</u> means to show that you
are not happy. **2.** To <u>cry</u> can also mean
to say something in a loud voice:
"Look out for the bear!" <u>cried</u> Tom.

D

demand   To <u>demand</u> something means
to ask for it in a very strong way:
"I want to go!" Jim <u>demanded</u>.

dinosaur   A <u>dinosaur</u> is an animal that lived long ago. Some <u>dinosaurs</u> were very big.

dough   If you mix flour and milk and some other things together, you will have <u>dough</u>. If you bake the <u>dough</u>, you will have bread.

E

enormous   If something is <u>enormous</u>, it is very big: An elephant is an <u>enormous</u> animal.

especially   If you like something <u>especially</u>, you like it most of all: Nan <u>especially</u> likes to draw dinosaurs.

expect   To <u>expect</u> something means
to think that it will happen:
We <u>expect</u> to win the ball game.

explain   When you <u>explain</u> something,
you tell about it: Mother <u>explained</u>
how to make bread.

F

favorite   If something is your <u>favorite</u>,
it is the one you like best:
My <u>favorite</u> color is blue.

flour   <u>Flour</u> is used to make
bread and other foods:
Father needs some <u>flour</u>
to make pancakes.

footprint   A footprint is a mark that is left by someone's foot: If you look at my footprints you will know where I walked.

foxy   To be foxy means to be smart: The hungry cat could not catch the foxy mouse.

G

ghost story   A ghost story is a scary story about ghosts and other make-believe things: I like to make up ghost stories to scare my friends.

grew   If something grew, it got bigger: The garden grew and grew.

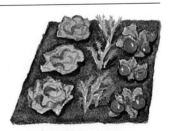

H

history When you study <u>history</u>,
you learn about the past: This <u>history</u>
book tells about life 100 years ago.

I

instead The word <u>instead</u> means
in place of: <u>Instead</u> of watching TV,
Jane read a book.

K

knock A <u>knock</u> is a tapping noise:
There was a <u>knock</u> at the door.

L

lead When you <u>lead</u>, you show the way
to go: Kim is <u>leading</u> her friends to the pond.

library   A <u>library</u> is a place where books are kept: Ana got two books from the <u>library</u>.

M

mill   A <u>mill</u> is a place where flour is made: Grandma always goes to the <u>mill</u> to buy flour.

minute   A <u>minute</u> is a short time: "Wait a <u>minute</u>," said Mary. "I want to go, too."

monster   A <u>monster</u> is a make-believe animal: I like scary stories about <u>monsters</u>!

N

nod   When you <u>nod</u> your head,
you move it up and down: Nan
<u>nodded</u> her head and said, "Yes."

notice   If you <u>notice</u> something, you
see it: Did you <u>notice</u> Ken's new coat?

O

orange   **1.** An <u>orange</u> is a kind of fruit:
I had an <u>orange</u> for lunch.
2. <u>Orange</u> is also the color of that
fruit: Bob has an <u>orange</u> hat.

P

pretty   If something is <u>pretty</u>, it is
nice to look at: Those flowers are very
<u>pretty</u>.

prize   A prize is something
you can win: Mother won
a prize for her drawing.

Q

quiet   If it is quiet, there is no noise:
You should be quiet in the library.

R

remember   To remember means
to think about something that
has happened: Sally remembered
the first day of school.

rise   **1.** To rise can mean to go up:
The sun rises in the morning.
2. To rise can also mean to get
bigger: The bread dough has to
rise, and then you can bake it.

ruin   To <u>ruin</u> something means to
make a mess of it: We forgot to water
the flowers. Now they are <u>ruined</u>!

S

sale   If something is for <u>sale</u>,
it means that people can buy it:
We are going to move, so our
house is for <u>sale</u>.

sew   When you <u>sew</u>, you use a
needle and thread: My button
fell off, but I <u>sewed</u> it back on.

sigh   To <u>sigh</u> means to let out a long
breath: Mark <u>sighed</u> and said, "I can't
find my book."

sign A <u>sign</u> is a board or a poster that tells something: Cars have to stop when they come to a stop <u>sign</u>.

stitch You make a <u>stitch</u> when you sew: Betty made some <u>stitches</u> to sew the two cloths together.

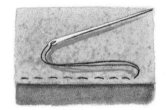

straight If you go <u>straight</u> to a place, you do not stop or go anywhere else: Ben went <u>straight</u> home.

suddenly If something happens <u>suddenly</u>, it happens very fast: <u>Suddenly</u> Lee jumped up and ran away!

T

tablecloth   A <u>tablecloth</u> is a
cloth used to cover a table:
"It's time to eat," said Father.
"Get the <u>tablecloth</u> and then
set the table."

terrible   Something that is <u>terrible</u> is
very bad: I have to clean up this
<u>terrible</u> mess!

true   Something that is <u>true</u> is real
— not make-believe: I will tell you
a <u>true</u> story.

turnip   A turnip is a vegetable
that grows under the ground:
We grow <u>turnips</u> and carrots
in our garden.

U

ugly Something that is <u>ugly</u> is not beautiful or pretty: We read a story about an <u>ugly</u> monster.

V

village A <u>village</u> is a small town: There is only one street in the tiny <u>village</u>.

visit To <u>visit</u> means to go see someone: Pam will <u>visit</u> her friend Sue.

W

well A <u>well</u> is a deep hole in the ground with water at the bottom: We went to the <u>well</u> to get some water.

wheat   Wheat is a plant that is used for food: This bread is made from wheat flour.

Y

year   A year is 12 months long: You have a birthday once a year.

Continued from page 2.

Credits

Cover Design: James Stockton & Associates.

Illustrators: 8–9 Lorinda Cauley
10–19 Jan Brett 20 Carol Schwartz
21–40 Dora Leder 41–54 Helen Oxenbury
55 Pat Hutchins 56–57 Maxie Chambliss
58–68 Derek Steele 69–87 Simms Taback
88 Christine Bassery 89 Wanda Gag
90–91 Lorinda Cauley 92–100 Arnold Lobel
101–111 Heather King 112–121 Robert L.
Crowe 122 David Rose 123 Steven Kellogg
124–125 Bill Bell 126–141 Nancy Edwards
Calder 142 Carol Inouye 143–152 Debbie
Holland 153 Tomie dePaola 156–157 Carol
Schwartz 158–177 Jack Kent 178–190 Gavin
Bishop 191 Donald Carrick 194–206 Aliki
207 Carol Inouye 208–217 Cathie Bleck
218–238 Bernard Waber 239 Eric Blegvad
240–241 Cheri Wyman 242–251 Rachel
Isadora 252–277 Barbara Douglass 278 Pat
Wong 279–298 Giulio Maestro 299 Trina
Schart Hyman

Photographers: 154–155 Kenneth W. Fink/
Bruce Coleman 192–193 Geoffrey Clifford/
Wheeler Pictures